# kids and drinking

# kids

# and drinking
## by Anne Snyder

Illustrations by
Susan Harlan

Published by

CompCare®
publications

Minneapolis, Minnesota
A division of Comprehensive Care Corporation

(Ask for our catalog. 800/328-3330, toll free outside
Minnesota or 612/559-4800. Minnesota residents.)

3      4      5      6

86    87    88    89

My love and gratitude to all the recovering alcoholic kids with whom I've been privileged to work.

And to kids everywhere who are faced with the question of drinking.

Anne Snyder

# Contents

**kids and drinking**

# Do you know that . . .

Alcohol is a drug?

Many children your age are alcoholics?

Alcoholism is a disease?

Alcoholism has nothing to do with being weak-willed or weak-minded?

It takes years of steady drinking for some adults to become alcoholic; it takes only months for kids?

There is help for young alcoholics. They can become happy and healthy again.

# Three stories

Sara, Kathy and Tommy are in their teens now, but they became full-blown alcoholics while they were still in elementary school.

They are real people. The stories you will read here are based on their own. But their names and some of the details have been changed to protect their identities.

They want to tell you their stories for two very good reasons: One, if you are having any problem as a result of alcohol, they would like you to know there is help for you. Two, they feel that the more you know about it, the better your choices will be concerning alcohol, now and in the future.

# Sara

# Sara

I was the second youngest in a family of seven kids, and the kind everyone picked on. I had nothing going for me; I wasn't pretty and I wasn't smart.

The first time I drank was the first time I forgot how lonely and different I felt.

One night, when I was nine, my thirteen-year-old sister — who was supposed to be babysitting me — took me to a party because she was stuck with me and didn't want to stay home.

When drinks were passed around, I took one. I hated the taste, but after a couple of shots I got high and staggered around making the kids laugh. I loved all the attention I got, so I acted drunker than I really was. Being the clown was fun . . . drinking was fun.

From then on, I hung around with the older kids. The bunch who appreciated how funny I was — the ones who were having the best time.

Our idea of fun was to get loaded, then knock over trash cans, teepee somebody's house or tree, or we'd hide on roofs of buildings and throw rocks. At this time, I never drank alone. Drinking meant having friends, and friends meant having to drink.

But before I was out of elementary school, I found I couldn't get along for a single day without drinking. I began going out with older boys . . . me, the ugly duckling. But I felt so uncomfortable that I couldn't handle it without either being drunk on booze or stoned on pills. When I was high, I felt pretty and loved . . . I forgot how really scared I always was on the inside.

The boys turned me on to pot, and between that and all the rest of the stuff, I was out of it most of the time. I started having hallucinations. I'd see things that weren't there. I'd hear echoes inside my head when I breathed . . . I'd be filled with these weird, crazy sounds . . . like a record player on the wrong speed. I liked feeling disconnected from the world . . . that way I couldn't hurt.

I became known as a stoner, and that made me feel important. But soon after that, I began to get sick. I tried to quit drinking. I couldn't. I was hooked.

I had to have money so I started to deal. I bought from the older kids and sold to the younger ones. I stole and I cheated . . . anything to get enough money to buy booze.

I did a lot of terrible things during this time, but I think the worst thing I ever did was to get my little sister onto alcohol and other drugs. I still feel ashamed and guilty about that.

I kept getting away with things. I'd sneak out of the house from my bedroom window when my parents were asleep and stay out half the night.

Once an older girl and I stole a car. She drove it smack into a police car. We had dope on us, we were under the influence, we had empty beer cans in the back, no driver's license . . . it's hard to believe, but I got off with just being out after curfew. I acted cute and I was so small that the cops must have felt sorry for us. They sobered us up and then called our parents.

My folks were pretty messed up themselves. My mom was drinking a lot; we kids were giving her plenty of trouble. I sure was doing more than my share. Once I heard her say she was going to kill herself, and I thought if she died it would be all my fault.

My mom and dad had awful fights. They'd blame each other every time one of us kids messed up. In the end, my father quit yelling at us and punishing us. He just stayed away from home most of the time.

Finally, my mom got to Alcoholics Anonymous and my dad went to Al-Anon — a group that helps families of alcoholics — but no matter what they said or did, I kept on doing my own thing.

I was getting pretty sick by now. I had terrific hangovers. I'd vomit my guts out and have the dry heaves. I became a blackout drinker and couldn't remember what happened for days at a time. What's really crazy is that I was still trying to convince myself I was having a good time.

My dad thought I was having emotional problems and talked me into going to an Alateen meeting. This is the group that helps kids of alcoholics. I met a girl there who I knew from school, and she asked me to come to an Alcoholics Anonymous meeting.

I was awful scared, but I went and I listened. I began to identify with the stories I heard; I knew then that I was an alcoholic. I found people there who cared, and they made me realize what I was doing to myself.

From that night, a year and a half ago, I haven't had a drink . . . or any other drug.

It wasn't easy getting sober. I had withdrawal cramps, couldn't sleep, had chills and shakes. But the AA people and my friend stuck with me and helped me over the worst of it.

After I felt better, I really began to live the AA program. I had a direction, a way to go. I did a lot of things I didn't like doing, but those were the things that helped me get well. I spoke up at AA meetings; I faced my bad attitudes and tried to change them; I took responsibility for my school work and behavior; I made amends to people I had hurt.

I can't believe how my life has turned around. After I'd been in AA for about six months, I began to get this weird feeling one night. I was in bed and suddenly felt like I was floating on a high, but I knew I was clean and sober. I laughed out loud when I realized what I was feeling was serenity . . . happiness . . . and I didn't know what it was because I'd never felt it before. That was the best trip I've ever been on, believe me.

Staying sober hasn't always been easy for me. Plenty of times I've been tempted to take a drink. But I wouldn't go back to the old way for anything.

I'm doing better at school and haven't been in any real trouble since I came to AA.

My little sister is still drinking, but I've told her my whole story, and I'm hoping she'll be willing to come to AA soon. I'm praying for that.

Now, it doesn't matter so much how I look or what other kids think of me. I still haven't got a lot of friends, but that's okay. The few I do have, I can trust. They like me for what I am.

Best of all, I like myself, too.

# Kathy

# Kathy

I was about seven years old when I first started drinking. I would taste my parents' drinks, and always finish what was left in the glasses after a party. Nobody cared. Sometimes they thought it was cute for a little kid like me to be drinking.

When I was eight years old, my mom and dad got divorced. They were both drinking pretty heavy then. My mother went off to another state and married three more times. My younger brother and I were left with my father.

My dad worked during the day and hit the bottle hard at night. It was up to me to keep an eye on my younger brother, and that made me mad. I was just as lonely and afraid as he was, but because I was the older one, I was ashamed to let anyone know how I felt.

I found out I felt better when I drank. I would sneak beer from the refrigerator. My dad would never know the difference.

By the time I was eleven, I was hanging around with older kids who drank beer and everything else they could get. For a while it was fun. But then I really started needing it.

I knew there was something different, even then, about the way I drank. The other kids did it just for kicks, but I had to have it all the time.

I started drinking hard liquor out of the bottle — even taking it to school with me. This was in elementary school. I'd put it in a coke can, my thermos, whatever.

Nobody knew how much I drank. I just couldn't tell anyone. I felt like a freak or something. But I held my feelings inside myself and that hurt me more. Mostly, I was afraid the kids around school would think I was weird.

It was awful when some of the kids found out about my drinking and made fun of me all the time. That made me drink even more. But when I was bombed, nothing bothered me. I went on like that for a long time.

Getting as much booze as I needed began to be a problem. When I couldn't get it anywhere else, I started stealing from my aunt and uncle, or other people. Sometimes I waited till my dad was asleep and took money from his wallet. I didn't want to steal, but I couldn't help myself. The more I drank, the more I needed to. I didn't know why I drank like that. All I knew is I didn't like how my life was, and it was a different world for me when I drank. It got so all I thought about was how to get the next drink.

Finally, I got caught drunk in school one day. They called my dad and I was sent home. He yelled at me and stuff like that, but that's all. I got put in a special class for problem kids.

After the trouble at school, I couldn't take my dad's liquor. But that didn't stop me — I'd steal from the drugstore or supermarket.

One night I got busted. They had mirrors and cameras at this store — that's how I got caught. I was sent to a rehabilitation center. That's a place for kids in trouble with the law.

15

It was at this place I first heard about Alcoholics Anonymous. Some people from AA came to talk to us, but I really didn't listen. When I got out of there, I just kept on drinking like before.

Then one day I passed out at school and was sent to the hospital. I hadn't been eating or sleeping much. I was pretty sick.

When I came out of the hospital, I was still feeling rotten. I was having withdrawal: stomach-aches, diarrhea, sweating. That came from stopping alcohol so suddenly. I was scared to drink and scared not to. I was really screwed up. What I did was cut down some.

About that time, my mom came back — not to live with us, but she was back in town. I guess she saw what was happening to me, and she asked me if I'd like to go to an AA meeting. I didn't know what else to do, so I said okay. I was so sick, I'd have said yes to anything.

For the first few months at AA, nothing made much sense to me. But one night a woman was talking, and she was telling **my** story. Not that she drank the same way I did, but she *felt* the same way I did. That blew my mind!

After that, I started to open up. I got the nerve to tell my mom all that happened to me. Then, once in a while, I'd talk at a meeting. It was slow, but I began to get better. It took me more than two years to stay sober for a straight six months.

At Alcoholics Anonymous they listened to you. It was a good feeling to know I wasn't the only one who got mixed up over booze. I didn't feel alone anymore. Nobody put me down or judged me. It was almost like the worse you were, the better they liked you.

And they laughed a lot at all the crazy things you had done. They didn't laugh *at* you, they laughed *with* you — and at themselves, too.

What I really liked was that I began to see some younger people at meetings — not a lot, but some. I found out we were practically all alike on the inside.

I started being the speaker at some meetings and going out to talk to kids at rehabilitation houses. Those kids were really messed up. They were not into reality — still pretty sick. But when they heard me talk about how I stopped drinking, some of them kind of listened. It gave me a great feeling to know that I could help somebody else.

Most kids were scared to tell anyone they were hooked on booze, just like I had been. They wouldn't even admit to themselves they had a problem. But if they did, they were on the way to getting well. That's the first step — admitting you have a problem.

If I told you all my troubles just went away when I got sober, I'd be lying. I'm fourteen now, and it's still rough at times. When I go to a party where kids are drinking, they sometimes make fun of me because I won't join in. It scares me a lot when I'm around people who drink, because I know if I take one sip I'm back where I started. I won't even take medicine if it has alcohol in it. I had to learn I don't have to be like everyone else. I can just be myself. If a party gets too wild, I can always leave.

It isn't easy, either, living with a father who is still drinking. He won't admit he's an alcoholic or that I am. He doesn't want me going to AA meetings. I tell my dad I'm sorry, but the only way I can live around here is to go to meetings and that's it.

Another problem is that my brother doesn't understand how it is with me. I tried to get him to go to Alateen — that's a group for the kids of alcoholics — but he's not interested. I'd like to slap him one when he says he's ashamed that I'm his sister because I'm a drunk. That hurts, but I have to let my brother and my dad find their own help in their own time. My job is to straighten *myself* out, not them.

I hate to see kids go through what I did — especially ten and eleven-year-olds — because that's how old I was when I got hooked.

When I was that age, I was alcoholic and didn't even know what the word meant. I didn't know alcohol was a drug. Now, I know if drinking changes any part of your life — like if you can't make it to school, or can't take part in some activity because of drinking — there's a good chance you're an alcoholic.

I wish elementary schools had some kind of a health class or science class that tells the alcoholic's side of the story. They could get us AA kids to come in and explain about alcoholism. If the kids in the class heard us and started asking questions, that would be a good breakthrough.

I got hooked on booze when I used it to relieve problems. But now I know that alcoholism is a disease — nothing to be ashamed of. It's like diabetes. It can't be cured but it can be controlled. Just as long as I don't take that first drink, I'll be okay.

I don't think enough people know or care that there are lots of little kids out there who are alcoholic.

I got help early. I was lucky.

# Tommy

# Tommy

I liked what alcohol did for me when I first tasted it. It kind of lifted my shyness and made me feel great.

I remember this wedding we went to. There was an open bar and I asked for Tom Collins for the adults and a coke for me. Then I took the whole tray and went to a table where there were older kids and drank my head off. I got very drunk and had to be carried home that night.

I was eight years old at the time.

From then on I sneaked drinks every chance I got. My mother drank very heavily, so there was plenty of stuff around all the time. Most of the time my mother was smashed and didn't know what was going on. Sometimes she'd be out cold on the floor. Other times my two sisters and I would have to fix ourselves a sandwich or something if we wanted to eat.

Our house was always like a crazy-house. My dad didn't drink, but he'd have a fight with my mother, and we kids would end up getting a beating. He was pretty violent.

There wasn't anyone I could talk to. My sisters and I fought a lot except when the three of us ganged up on my mother.

Once I threatened to tell my father just how much mom drank, and she threw a book at me. When the teacher asked me about my black eye the next day, I said my sister beat me up.

I was always dressed sloppy and wasn't eating right, so when I was in third grade a teacher sent me to this place called a Mental Health Clinic. I told the people what was going on at home, but nothing was done about it. After a while I stopped going there.

One night my mother got really bombed and started throwing things around. My sisters and I were scared, so we all ran out and went to my grandmother's house.

My grandma got in touch with Alcoholics Anonymous. Some people came to talk to my mother and took her to a place to dry her out for a week.

When she came home things were better, but she'd always be going out to these AA meetings. I resented that — I wanted her home with me.

I felt lonely and scared. But I'd take a drink and feel better right away. And when we went to parties or to grandma's house — any place drinks were served — I always found a way to sneak a drink or two.

As I got older I drank even more. It was very easy to get booze. You'd just go to the store and wait for someone around eighteen to buy it for you. Everybody did it; even the school athletes had hidden bottles at the Saturday night dances.

I think I was a full-blown alcoholic by that time, but I didn't know it. All I knew was that I lived for that next drink.

It was funny that my parents never caught on. If I was too drunk to go home, I'd say I was sleeping over at someone's house. I learned all kinds of ways to keep my parents from knowing the truth.

Right from the beginning, I always drank more than anybody else. I tried different drugs, but they didn't turn me on like booze did. I always carried a little bottle in my pocket at school. Then if I had to do a speech or participate in class I'd feel okay. The teachers praised me for being outgoing. It was great.

Booze was never discussed at school. The big thing was drugs. The teachers talked about nothing else. One time we did see a movie about alcohol, but it was like five minutes long. No one bothered to talk about it afterwards.

When I got to high school, my drinking was out of control. Twice, I got picked up for drunk driving, but somehow I got off. I'd wake up sometimes and not remember what had happened the night before. That was scary. It blew my mind. And I was running out of friends. The kids were getting sick of my being a falling-down drunk.

I tried to knock it off. Some days I didn't drink at all — but I felt rotten just the same. I decided I was better off drunk. I couldn't sleep much, and when I did, I'd wake up with my arms and legs jerking with tremors.

I took jobs as a grocery carry-out boy to get drinking money, but most of the time I'd quit as soon as I had money in my pocket. Or I'd show up drunk and get fired.

Then I decided there was something wrong in my head; I really didn't think the problem was drinking. So I went to a psychiatrist. I didn't level about how much I drank, and he gave me pills. Now I was on pills *and* booze. He advised me to quit drinking but never said how to quit. He just said if I was drinking not to bother to come in.

I quit the psychiatrist and started drinking day and night and didn't care who knew it. I'd drink until I passed out, then wake up and start over again. If I ran out of money, I'd steal the booze I needed. And if I couldn't do that, I'd take my mother's charge plate and get a gift certificate. Then I'd go to the other window and say I couldn't find what I wanted and get the cash.

By now, I'd drink all alone so nobody would bother me. I made a room out of the cellar of our house and could come in and out without anyone knowing. My parents had no idea what I was doing. I felt terrible. I wanted to die. It got so I couldn't get drunk and I couldn't get sober. We lived in Seattle then.

Finally, I heard about this therapy and decided to go there. That didn't work out either; I just kept going downhill. I threatened to bomb the therapy place. They called the police, but I wasn't held. I just said I had been taking prescribed pills and had a bit too much to drink. Even when I OD'd a couple of times, they just pumped out my stomach and released me. I'd give them a song-and-dance about how it was accidental. My parents were called finally, and they came and took me back home.

I heard about this detox center where they dry you out — and I went over there to check in. I changed my mind when I saw bars on the windows, but it was too late. I had already been admitted. I had a bottle down in my pants, and I started a big commotion. I put up a battle, but five men carried me off. There I was, and there I stayed for two weeks.

I thought I'd go crazy the first few days, but then I cooled off and looked and listened to the other patients. There were kids who looked middle-aged; some insane from drinking; some looked ready to die. I wanted to run but we were locked up like in jail.

Members of Alcoholics Anonymous came to talk to us and for once in my life I paid attention. We had regular AA meetings and learned about the Twelve Step program. I knew then that I'd either change or die.

When I got out, I went back home and the first thing I did was call AA. That was about five months ago.

I've had one slip, but I'm doing okay now. And I have a lot of hope. I'm scared, but I'm trying to live one day at a time the AA way. Just for today, I don't have to drink.

I have a sponsor and I'm going to meetings every day. I'm getting to know other kids on the program, and some of their stories are a lot worse than mine.

I guess if they can get sober, I can make it, too. That's what I'm praying for. They say you have to be willing to go to any lengths to get sobriety.

I'm willing.

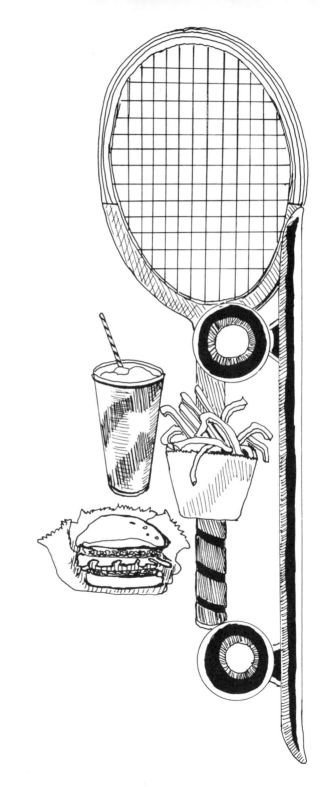

# Twenty
# Questions

This is not a school quiz. You will not be graded. Take this short test and find out how your drinking is affecting *you*.

# Twenty questions

☐ ☐   1. Are you ever absent from school because of drinking?

☐ ☐   2. Do you need a drink to make you feel better around other people?

☐ ☐   3. Do you ever hide your beer, liquor, or wine?

☐ ☐   4. Do you feel braver when you drink . . . less afraid?

☐ ☐   5. Do you ever drink alone?

☐ ☐   6. Do you drink as a way to stop worrying?

☐ ☐   7. Do you feel guilty about your drinking?

☐ ☐   8. Do you get upset when anyone says you drink too much?

☐ ☐   9. Is it necessary for you to drink in order to have fun?

☐ ☐  10. Does drinking make you feel more equal to the other kids?

☐ ☐  11. Do you sneak drinks from your parents' supply or anyone else's?

☐ ☐  12. Did you ever steal money to buy beer, liquor, or wine?

☐ ☐  13. Did you ever steal beer, liquor, or wine?

☐  ☐  14. Have you stayed away from the "straight" kids since you started drinking?

☐  ☐  15. Do you mostly hang around with the kids who drink?

☐  ☐  16. Do most of your friends drink less than you do?

☐  ☐  17. Do you drink until you are drunk or until the bottle is done?

☐  ☐  18. Have you ever forgotten what happened while you were drinking?

☐  ☐  19. Have you ever been busted or had any medical treatment because of drinking?

☐  ☐  20. Do you think you have a drinking problem?

—  —  TOTALS

If you answered **Yes** to any one question, this could be a warning that you are a problem drinker. If you answered **Yes** to any two, chances are you might be **an alcoholic.** If you answered **Yes** to three or more, you probably are **an alcoholic.**

# Questions and answers about alcoholism

# Questions and answers about alcoholism

### What is alcoholism?

Alcoholism is a disease. It is a progressive disease. If not treated, it can only get worse, never better. It is a lifetime disease. Alcoholics cannot control their drinking once they start, even after years of not drinking. Alcoholism can cause insanity and death. Alcoholics are apt to have fatal accidents. Sometimes they commit suicide because they feel so frightened and hopeless. Or they get sick with other illnesses because they don't take care of themselves.

### Can alcoholism be cured?

Alcoholism cannot be cured, but it can be stopped. The only known way to stop the disease is for the alcoholic to totally quit drinking alcohol in any form. Alcoholics can be helped. They can live normal, productive, and happy lives if their disease is recognized and treated.

### Who are alcoholics?

Anyone can be an alcoholic. Most alcoholics are

not "bums." The disease can affect anyone; young or old, rich or poor, male or female. If drinking affects any part of a person's life — whether at school, at play, at work, or at home — there is a good possibility that person is alcoholic.

## Why can't the alcoholic just stop drinking?

The alcoholic believes he or she can't live without drinking. This is an *obsession.* Alcoholics drink to escape physical or emotional pain. When some alcoholics try to quit drinking, the withdrawal symptoms are so severe that they drink to relieve the pain. This is *addiction.* **Alcohol is a drug!**

Most alcoholics would like to drink like other people, but once they start they usually end up drunk. This is *compulsion.*

## Who can stop the alcoholic from drinking?

Nobody can force the alcoholic to stop drinking. *The desire to stop drinking must be the choice of the alcoholic, only.* But he or she can be helped. Alcoholics Anonymous (AA) is the most success-ful group known to help alcoholics who want to be helped.

# What is an alcoholic?

# What is an alcoholic?

Alcoholics cannot predict when or how much they will drink. Sometimes they will not drink for weeks or months, but when they do take that first drink, they will continue whether they want to or not. This is called *loss of control.*

Alcoholics may not drink greater amounts, but they become drunk more often as time goes by. They begin to depend more and more on alcohol to be able to go through their daily activities. This is called *progression.*

When alcoholics try to stop drinking, they could suffer from nausea and vomiting, cramps, headaches, and shaking. They may have double vision or even "see things." This is called delirium tremens or DT's. At times, the alcoholic may go into convulsions and require hospital care. All these effects are called *withdrawal symptoms.*

Alcoholics behave in a very different manner when they are drinking than when they are sober. This is called *personality change.*

Alcoholics can sometimes go through experiences, and then truly not remember what they did or said. At times this can last for entire days or weeks. *These are called blackouts.*

If you have any questions about your own drinking, or if you would like any more information about Alcoholics Anonymous, please contact your local AA in the phone book. Or contact:

Alcoholics Anonymous World Services, Inc.
Box 459, Grand Central Station,
New York, NY 10017

You may also find help by contacting your local
Council on Alcoholism.

If you live in a good-sized city, you can look in
your phone book under "alcohol" or "alcoholism"
and usually find an alcohol information or referral
center. Do you know the names of alcoholism
treatment centers near you? Is there a CareUnit
nearby? Call them; they can tell you where to go
and what to do first.

# Remember!

An alcoholic is not
good or bad —
but sick!

Alcoholism
has nothing to do
with will power
or intelligence!

# Parent/Teacher Guide

# Parent/Teacher Guide

All over the country, alcoholism among elementary school children is surfacing.

In one California county alone, a survey indicated that 85 percent of the students over age seven drink alcohol, at least occasionally . . . 29 percent use other drugs, either in combination with alcohol or alone.

More and more children are turning from other drugs to alcohol. The reasons are simple. 1. It is easy to obtain. 2. It is cheap. 3. It is legal. 4. It is socially acceptable.

**It takes years of steady drinking for some adults to become alcoholic. It takes only months for their juvenile counterparts!**

One of the ways in which we may effectively **prevent** alcohol abuse is to expose the myths surrounding alcohol.

The following are suggestions for use in the schoolroom and / or home:

1. Discuss the use of alcohol in stories on TV and film. When the hero gets the girl, what does he do? When he loses the girl? When he gets promoted? Gets fired? Can the student recall other such instances seen on the screen?

2. Discuss the "glamous image" imposed upon the public regarding drinking, i.e.: the two-fisted hero who can "hold his liquor like a man;" the romantic wine-drinking couple; young people frolicking on the beach with friends **and** beer.

3. Discuss drinking habits of students' own families and friends.
4. Discuss students' first taste of alcohol. What were the circumstances? What effect did it have on the student?
5. Discuss students' own opinions regarding drinking.
6. Questions for discussion: How does the student handle fear? Loneliness? Frustration? What are constructive escapes? What are destructive escapes?
7. Have a young AA member come to the classroom to talk to the children and answer questions.
8. Arrange a field trip to visit an open AA meeting if possible.
9. Circulate pamphlets describing Alcoholics Anonymous, Al-Anon, and Alateen.
10. Discuss what action the student can take if he or she finds himself hooked on alcohol. What can the student do if a member of the family or a friend is alcoholic?

To learn more about young people and alcohol, please write:

CompCare Publications,
Box 27777
Minneapolis Minnesota 55427

# About the author

Anne Snyder has been involved in a variety of writing jobs, including fiction, nonfiction, records, and films.

A teacher of creative writing, Ms. Snyder first wrote *50,000 Names for Jeff*, published by Holt, Rinehart and Winston, Inc. The story of a black child's single-handed fight against discrimination in housing, the book was named as one of the ten best books of the year by the Child Studies Association of America. It was reprinted in the Owlet edition by Holt.

Regarded as a bibliotherapeutic specialist in contemporary literature for children and young adults, Ms. Snyder also wrote *Nobody's Family*, an adventure story dealing with Mexican children and the problem of illegal aliens.

*First Step*, in both hard cover and paperback (Signet New American Library), won the coveted top juvenile writing award by the Friends of American Writers in 1976, and was honored by the National Council of Christians and Jews as a brotherhood book. This is the widely praised story of a teenager trapped in an alcoholic home, and was received with glowing reviews.

Other juvenile novels by Anne Snyder include, *Counterplay*, *Two Point Zero*, *Good-bye, Paper Doll*, and *My Name is Davy — I'm an Alcoholic*, now translated into Danish and Finnish. All of these are slated for production as special movies for television. *Good-bye, Paper Doll,* a teenage love story in which the young heroine is a victim of anorexia nervosa, will be aired as an ABC-TV after-school special.

Ms. Snyder, a TV script writer too, also authored a documentary film, *New Beginnings: Women, Alcohol, and Recovery.*

She lives in Woodland Hills, California and is a member of Writers Guild of America, Authors League, Southern Council of Literature for Children and Young People, Women's National Book Association, Inc., PEN International, and the Society of Children's Book Writers.

# From CompCare Publications:
## for young people and the adults who care about them

**. . . But I Didn't Make Any Noise About It,** The Story of My Teenage Son's Drug Dependency, by Cindy Lewis-Steere. The author of *Stepping Lightly* brings hope to all parents of young drug- and alcohol-abusers in this moving account of her own family's crisis and painful growth. Her open sharing of feelings and solutions illustrates very clearly that as the entire family is affected by one member's drug problem, the family also must be part of the recovery. This pamphlet, recommended by counselors, is used by parent and family groups, as well as by individual families. *Pamphlet.*

**Haunted Inheritance** by Lucy Barry Robe. Illustrated by Mimi Noland. A mystery with a message skillfully weaves in the truth that alcoholism is a disease and is treatable. This brisk story in an elegant setting contains important information for junior high school ages up. (Adults like it, too!) *Illustrated paperback.*

**I Never Saw the Sun Rise** by Joan Donlan. A high school counselor says: "This book should be required reading for every high school student in the country — and for all parents." A rare, as-it-happened journal by a talented 15-year-old writer and artist tells of her drug dependency, her treatment, and her recovery; offers important insights to teens and parents that can help prevent youth drug and alcohol problems. *Paperback, illustrated by the author.*

**If Only My Family Understood Me** by Don Wegscheider. Foreword by Virginia Satir. Teenage readers and parents, too, with stressful problems in their families may see themselves in this easy-to-understand book — in the role of Victim, Caretaker, Protector, Family Pet, Problem Child, or Forgotten Child. The same insights, so helpful to troubled families, can help any family (troubled or not) have more fun living together. *Illustrated paperback.*

**Just So It's Healthy,** New Evidence That Drinking and Drugs Can Harm Your Unborn Baby, by Lucy Barry Robe. Foreword by Stanley E. Gitlow, M.D. Now in language easily understood by everyone from high school students to health professionals, here are medical and scientific facts that could make the difference between a healthy, strong baby and one born with physical and/or mental defects. Every family should be aware of Fetal Alcohol Syndrome (FAS), symptoms which may be seen in babies of drinking (even moderately drinking) mothers. *Paperback.*

**Mom, How Come I'm Not Thin?** by Bill and Enid Bluestein, illustrated by Susan Kennedy. Especially for ages 7 to 11. Winner of the Brandeis University Library Trust Award for Achievement in Children's Literature. Any overweight child who feels left behind in a thin world will find comfort in this gentle, sensitively illustrated story about 10-year-old Dolly. Pediatricians and counselors have welcomed this book, as have hundreds of frustrated parents of chubby children, who find it's the long-needed answer to that question sometimes too painful to be asked out loud, "Mom, how come I'm not thin?" *Hardcover, picture book format.*

**The Year Santa Got Thin** by Enid and Bill Bluestein. A modern folktale in high-spirited rhyme, for all ages for all seasons, tells how roly poly Santa decides to change his shape and his image. This tall *thin* tale about pride and pudginess appeals at many levels as it smuggles in some good information about losing weight, vanity, and tampering with traditions. Brilliantly illustrated by Joe Pearson, this is a perfect gift for a family — yours or a friend's. *Hardcover, picture book format.*

**Young Alcoholics** by Tom Alibrandi. A youth counselor takes a realistic look at adolescent alcoholism in this country in a straight-talking book for parents and other concerned adults, as well as for teens. Statistics show that over a million 12-to-17-year-olds in the United States have serious drinking problems and that the use and abuse of alcohol has spread downward to gradeschool ages. Tests to show if a youngster is in trouble — or headed for trouble — with alcohol are included. *Paperback.*

All of the above books are published by and available from CompCare Publications. None is either endorsed or opposed by the author of this book. Ask us to send you a free CompCare Publications catalog of quality books and other materials emphasizing a positive approach to life's problems for young people and adults on a broad range of topics. If you have questions, call us toll free at 800/328-3330. (Minnesota residents: Call 612/559-4800.)